the first summer study book for violin

by cassia harvey

CHP186

©2007 by C. Harvey Publications All Rights Reserved.
www.charveypublications.com - print books
www.learnstrings.com - PDF downloadable books
www.harveystringarrangements.com - chamber music

Violin Note Chart

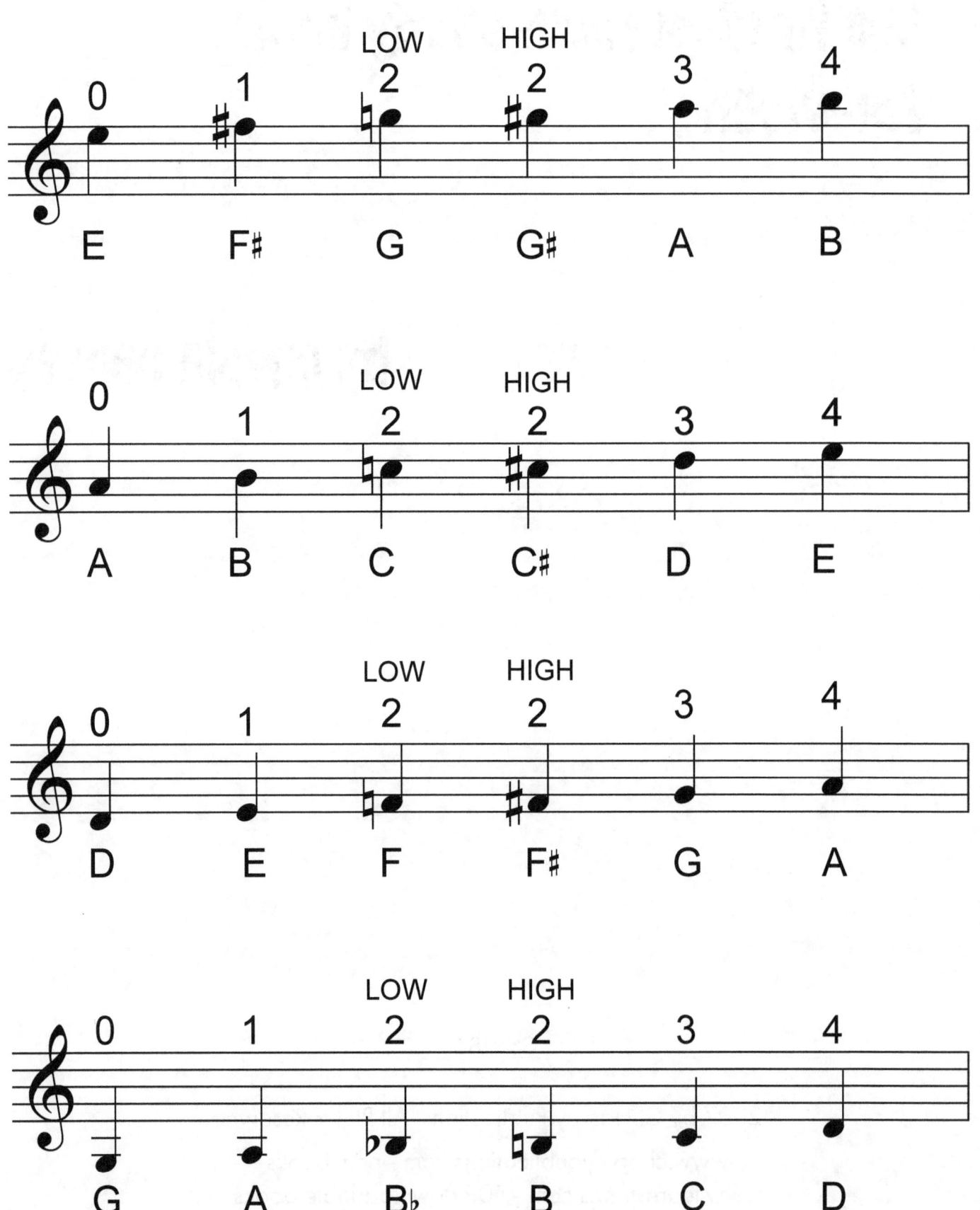

©2007 C. Harvey Publications All Rights Reserved.

1. No more flimsy first fingers!

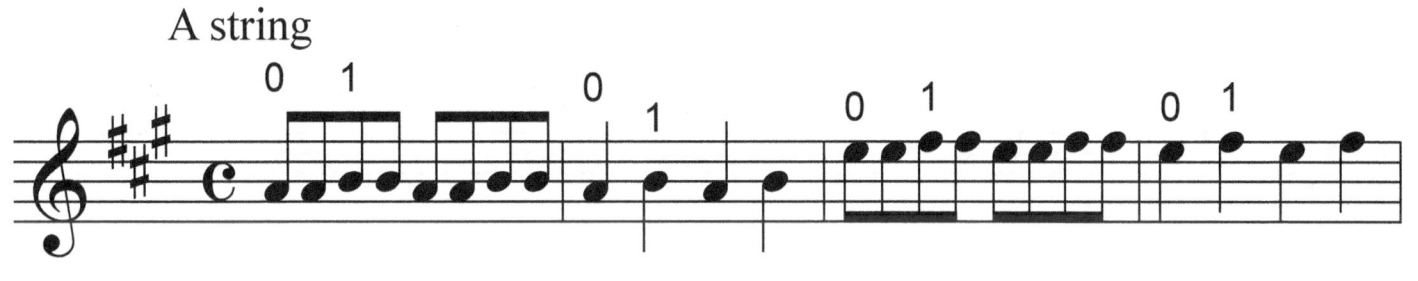

2. Cripple Creek

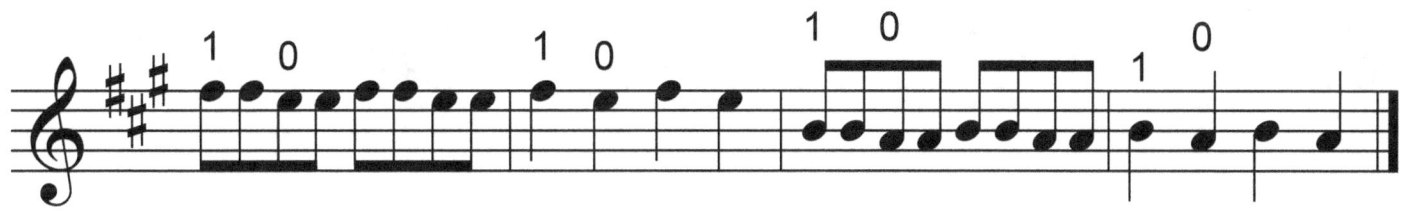

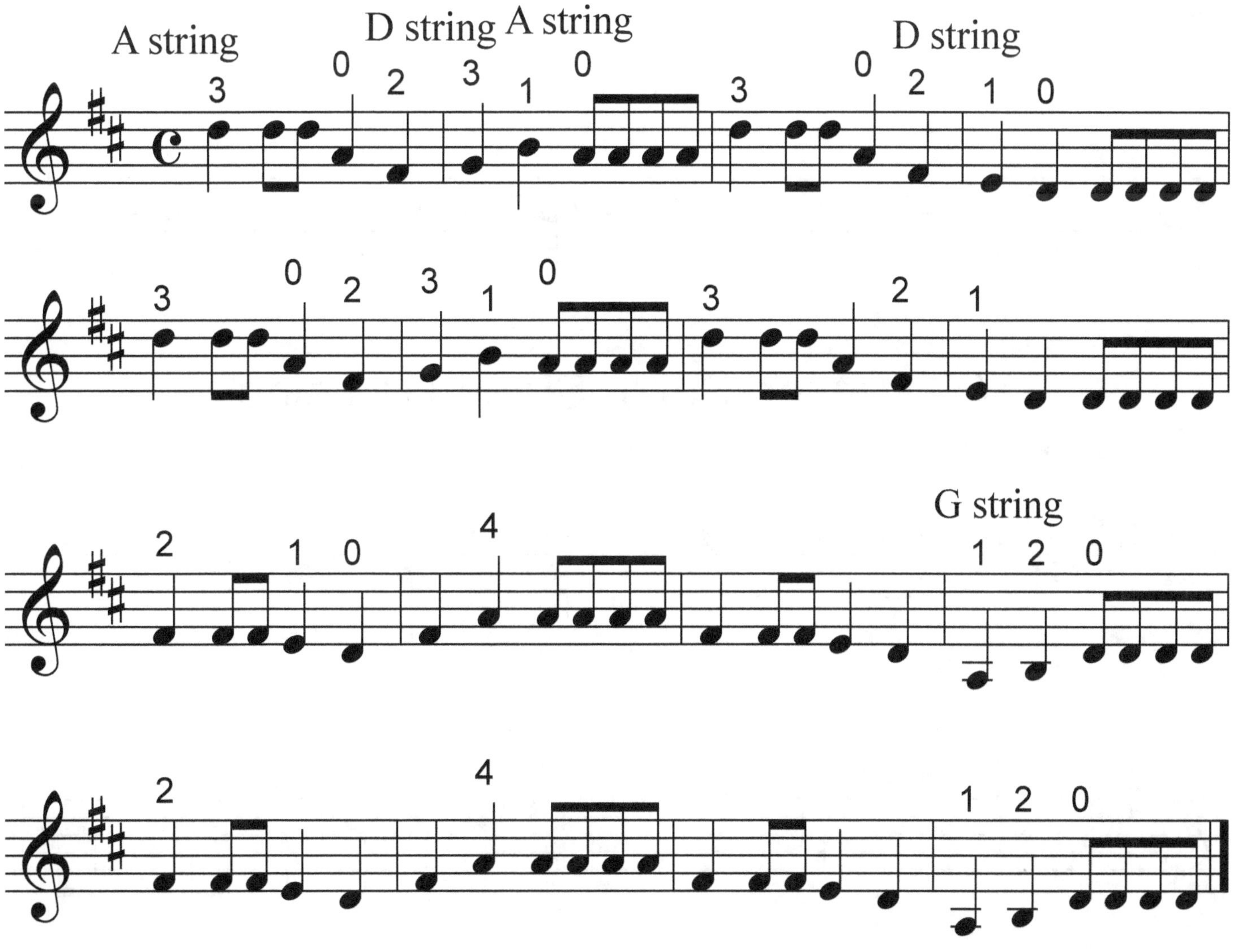

3. What Do You Do With a Drunken Sailor?

4. Drunken Sailor String Crossing

5. Fiddle Tune

6. Rossini's William Tell

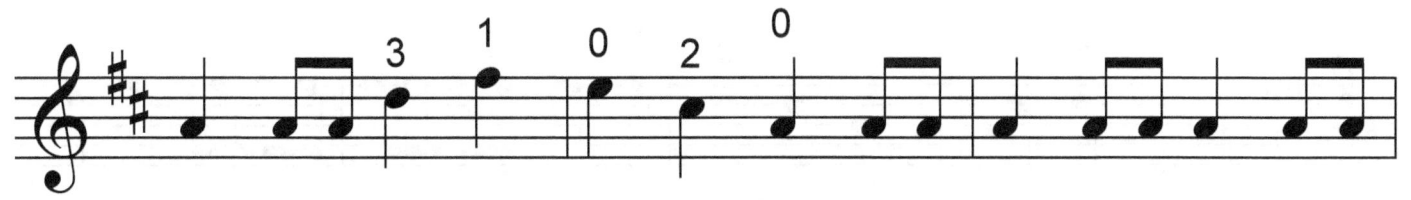

9. Oh Susannah

A string

Foster/arr. Harvey

10. Susannah's Exercise

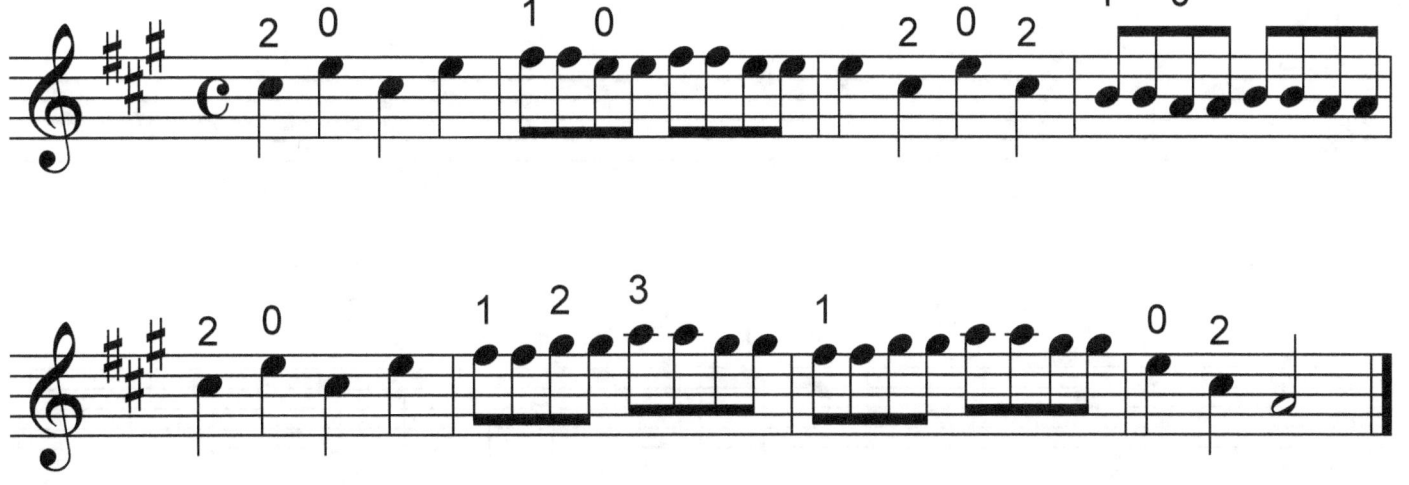

©2007 C. Harvey Publications All Rights Reserved.

11. Mountain Exercise

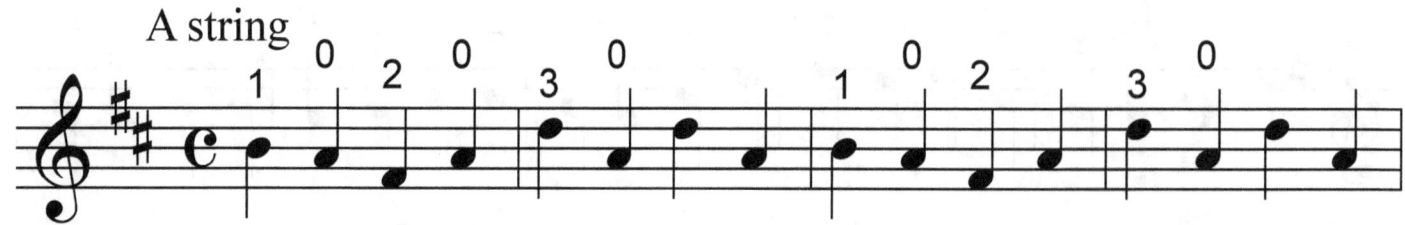

12. She'll Be Comin' Round the Mountain

©2007 C. Harvey Publications All Rights Reserved.

13. Sleep Exercise

14. Are You Sleeping?

15. Sleeping Yet?

©2007 C. Harvey Publications All Rights Reserved.

16. Finger Trainer

17. Michael, Row the Boat Ashore

©2007 C. Harvey Publications All Rights Reserved.

18. Find the Hidden Songs

19. Bugler's Exercise

20. Reveille Bugle Call

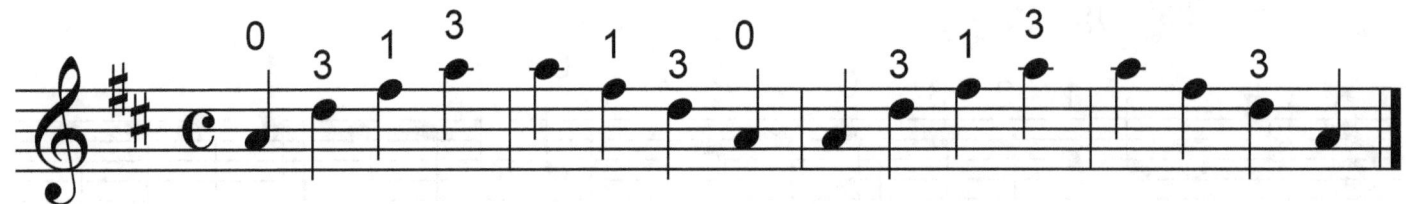

21. Bugler's Next Exercise

22. Assembly Bugle Call

22. Taps Bugle Call

Remember: A dotted half note gets 3 counts.

©2007 C. Harvey Publications All Rights Reserved.

23. Finger Running

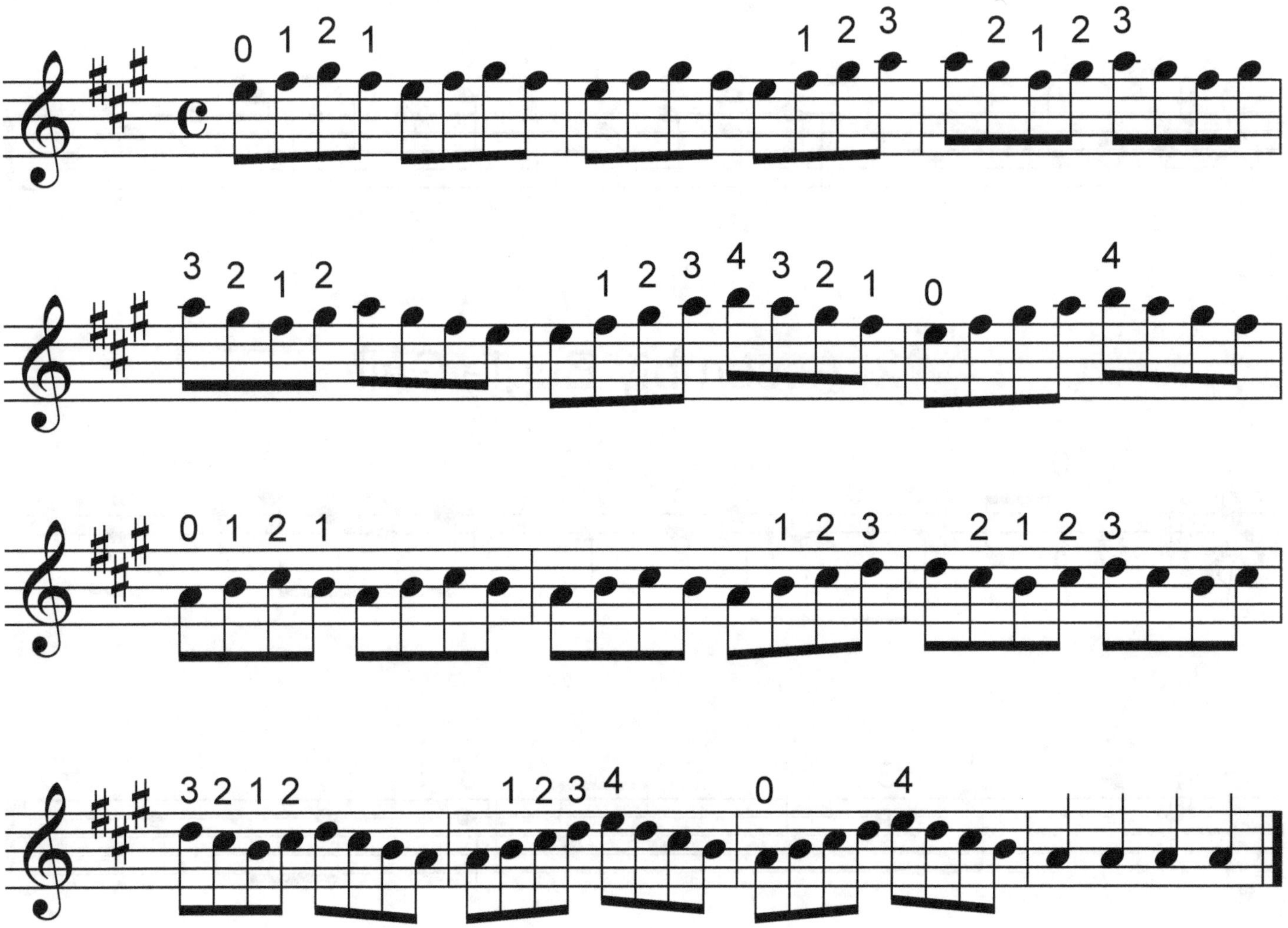

24. Swallowtail Jig

©2007 C. Harvey Publications All Rights Reserved.

25. Playing on G and D

26. Buffalo Gals

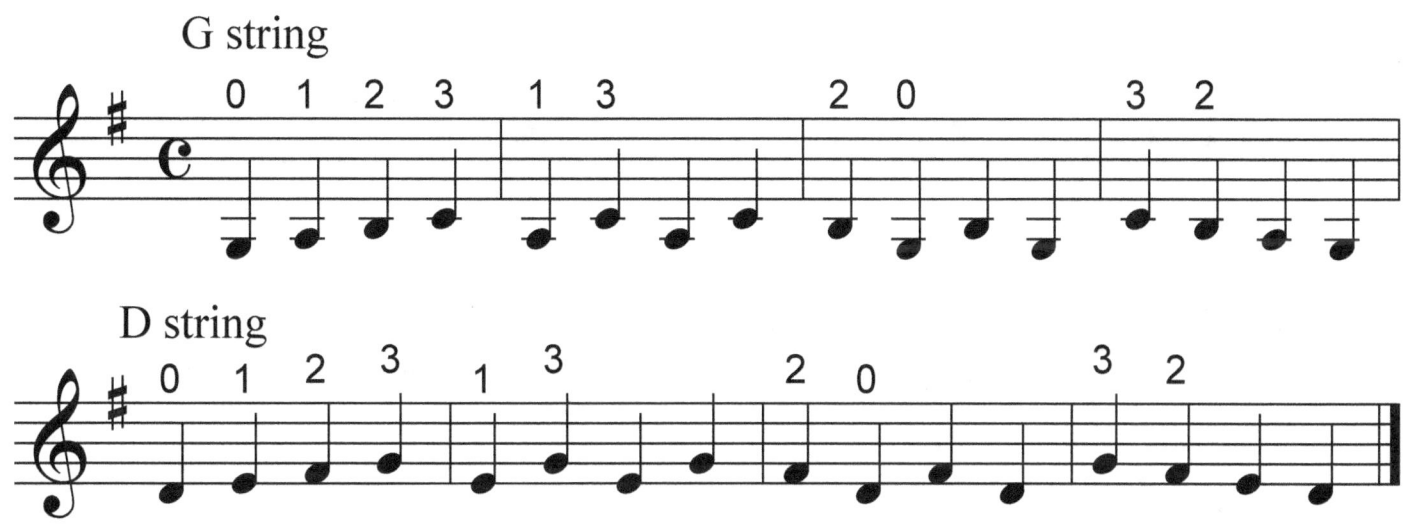

28. Arpeggios

29. On Top of Old Smoky

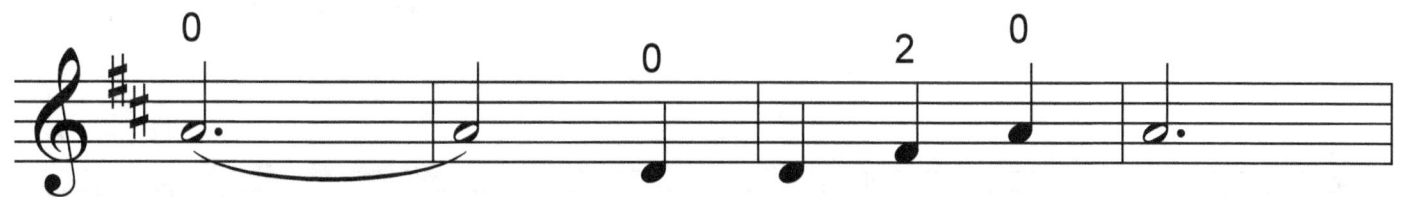

©2007 C. Harvey Publications All Rights Reserved.

32. This Old Man

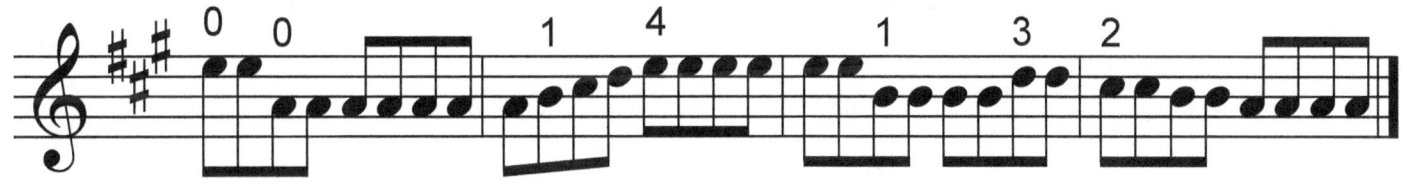

33. Double Trouble

©2007 C. Harvey Publications All Rights Reserved.

34. String Crossing

35. Simple Gifts

©2007 C. Harvey Publications All Rights Reserved.

36. Using the 4th Finger

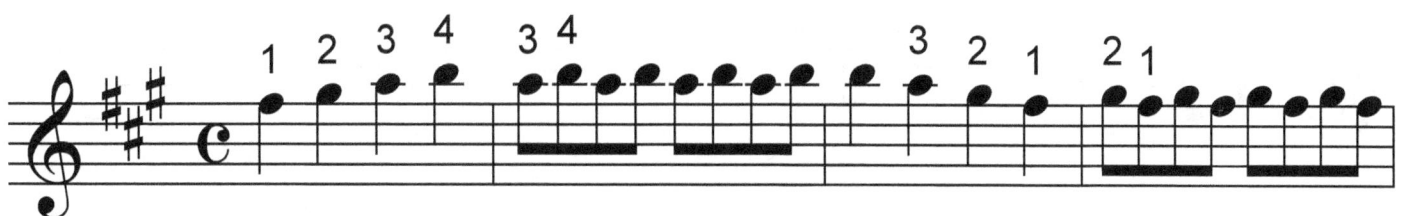
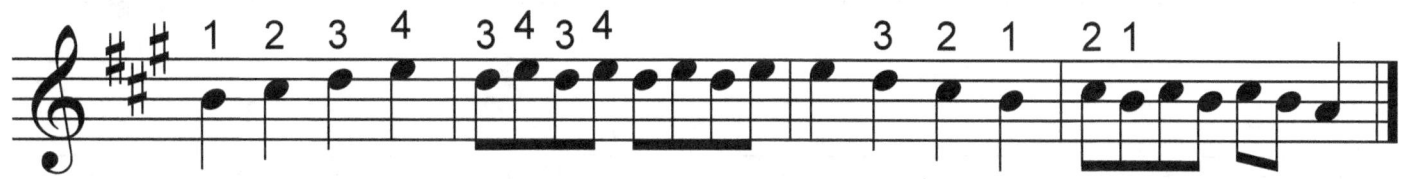

37. Battle Cry of Freedom

Root/arr. Harvey

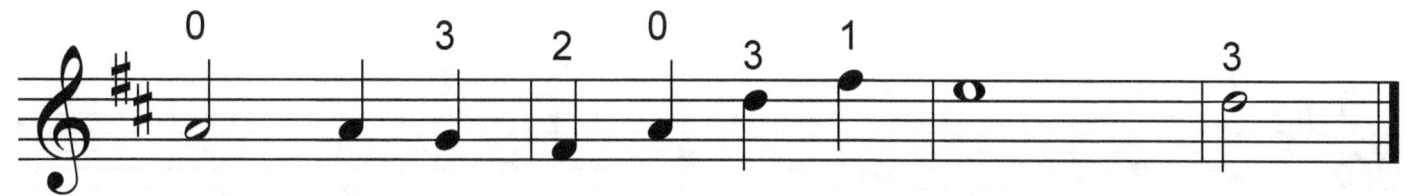

40. Home on the Range

Kelley/arr. Harvey

©2007 C. Harvey Publications All Rights Reserved.

41. Hail to the Chief

Sanderson/arr. Harvey

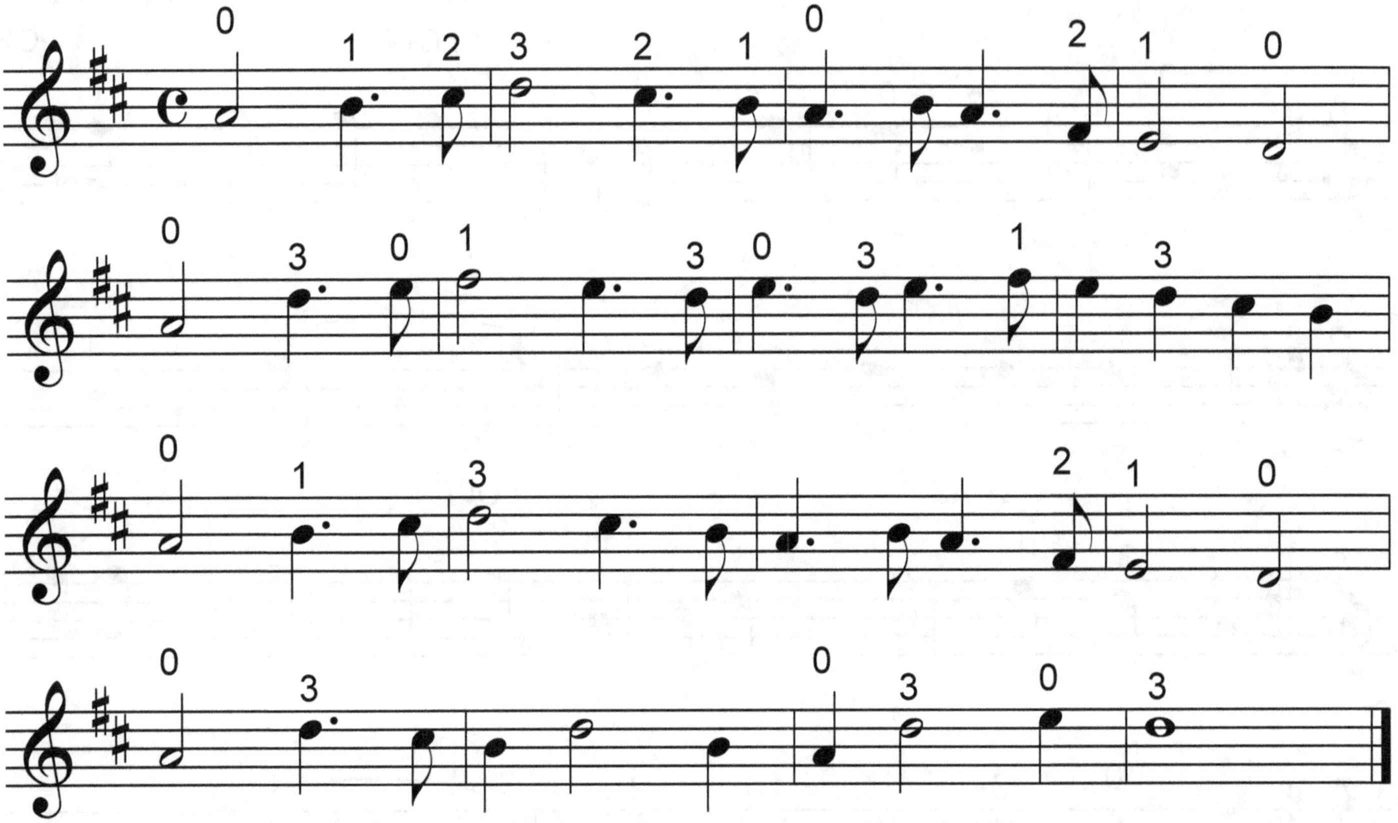

42. Yankee Doodle

A string

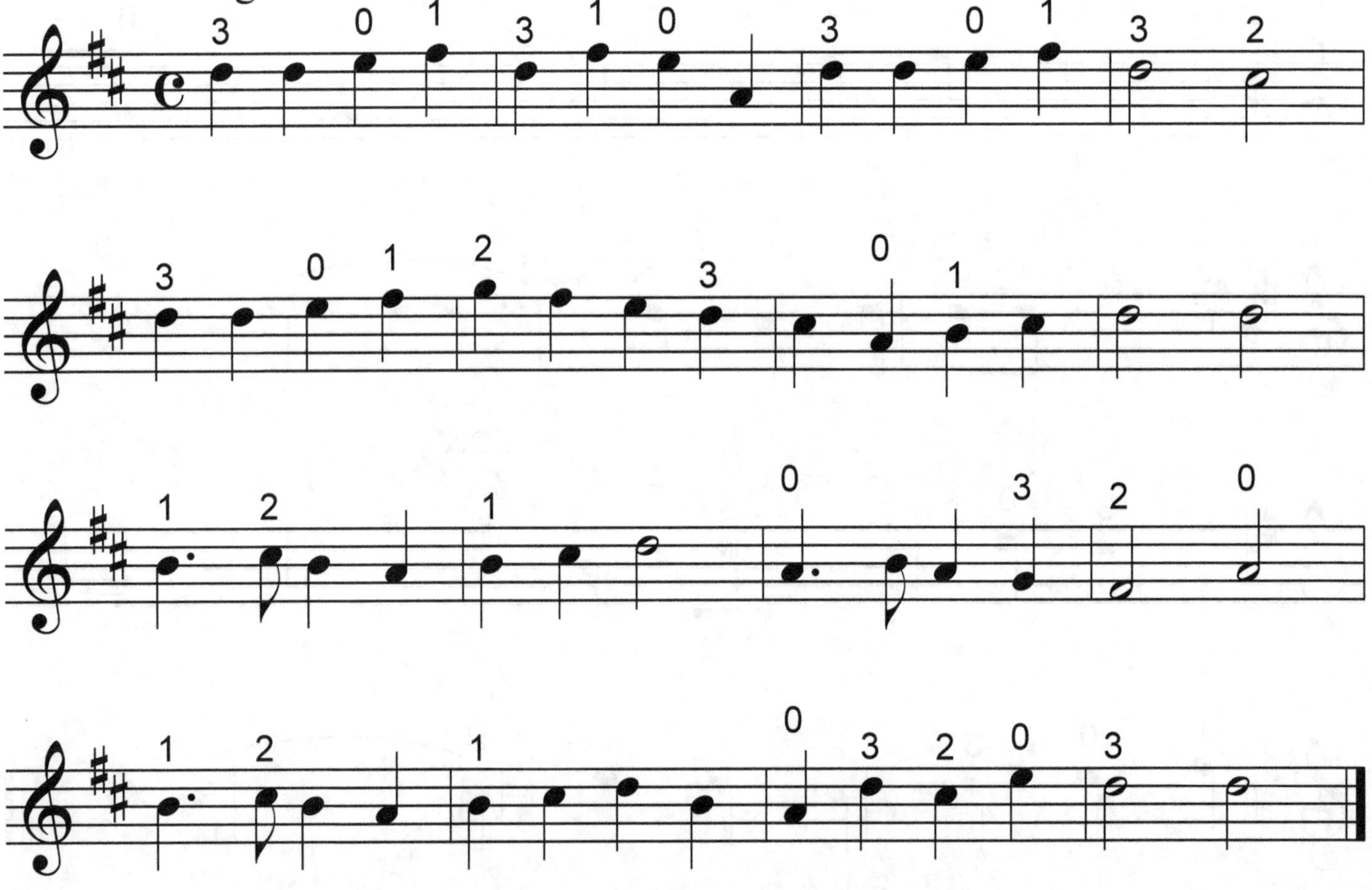

available from **www.charveypublications.com**: CHP303

Beginning Fiddle Duets for Two Violins

Cripple Creek

Trad., arr. Myanna Harvey

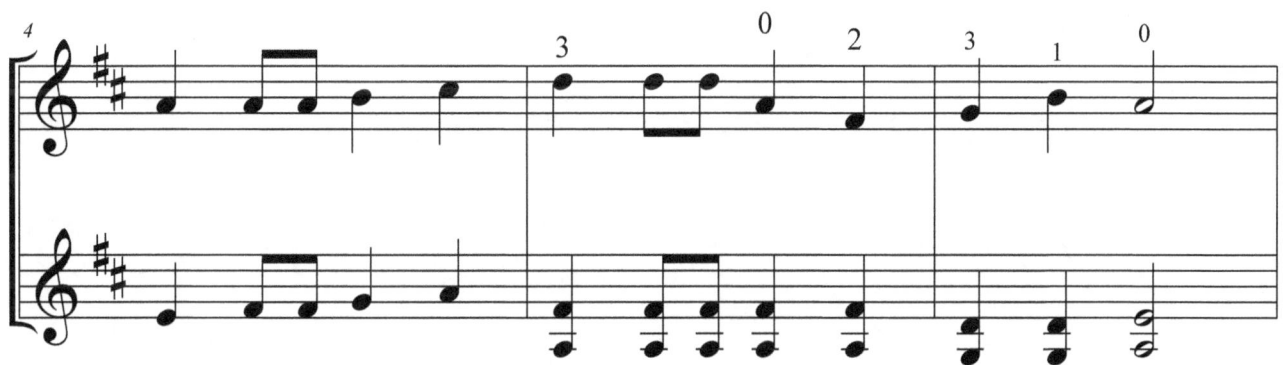

©2016 C. Harvey Publications All Rights Reserved.